SEEING THEIR PREY
ANIMALS WITH AN AMAZING SENSE OF SIGHT

written by Kathryn Lay
illustrated by Christina Wald

magic
Wagon

visit us at www.abdopublishing.com

Published by Magic Wagon, a division of the ABDO Group, PO Box 398166, Minneapolis, MN 55439.

Printed in the United States of America, North Mankato, Minnesota.
052012
092012

 This book contains at least 10% recycled materials.

Written by Kathryn Lay
Illustrated by Christina Wald
Edited by Stephanie Hedlund and Rochelle Baltzer
Cover and interior layout and design by Neil Klinepier

Library of Congress Cataloging-in-Publication Data

Lay, Kathryn.
  Seeing their prey : animals with an amazing sense of sight / written by Kathryn Lay ; illustrated by Christina Wald.
     p. cm. -- (Sensing their prey)
  Includes index.
  ISBN 978-1-61641-867-0
  1. Vision--Juvenile literature. 2. Senses and sensation--Juvenile literature. 3. Animal behavior--Juvenile literature.
I. Wald, Christina, ill. II. Title.
  QP475.7.L39 2013
  573.8'8--dc23
                         2011052276

CONTENTS

Can You See Your Dinner?

Animals must find their own food every day. A predator is an animal that lives by eating other animals. Predators have strong senses that help them. Many use their sense of sight to search for their prey.

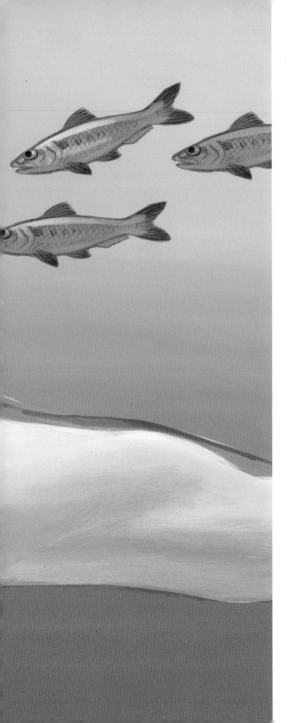

Some predators have special features that help them see. These features can help them find their prey from far away or at night. They can even see what color it is.

LONG-DISTANCE DINNER

The golden eagle sits high on a rock or a tree or flies over the land. From there, it can see a rabbit from one mile (1.6 km) away.

Could you see your food if it was a mile (1.6 km) away? Two miles (3.2 km) away? Could you see your favorite restaurant from the other side of town?

A vulture finds its prey by using telescopic vision. It does not locate its food by smelling it. The vulture usually finds carrion before it begins to rot and stink.

Crocodiles also have strong eyesight on land. They cannot see well underwater because a film covers their eyes for protection. This transparent eyelid slides back above water, so crocodiles can see their prey from far away on land.

Lens

Cornea

Retina

Mirror

SEEING FOOD IN THE DARK

Nocturnal predators, such as owls, hunt at night. They have special mirrorlike shapes in the back of their eyes. They also have larger pupils and complex retinas. These things all help the animal see in the dark.

Deep-sea animals have the same features in their eyes as nocturnal animals. The brownsnout spookfish looks like it has four eyes. Instead, it has two that are split into different parts. One half looks up while the other half looks down into the dark water. This way the fish can see flashes of light coming from its prey.

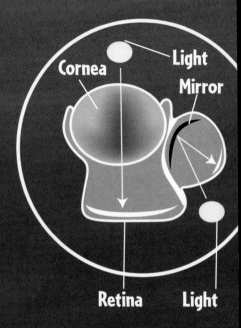

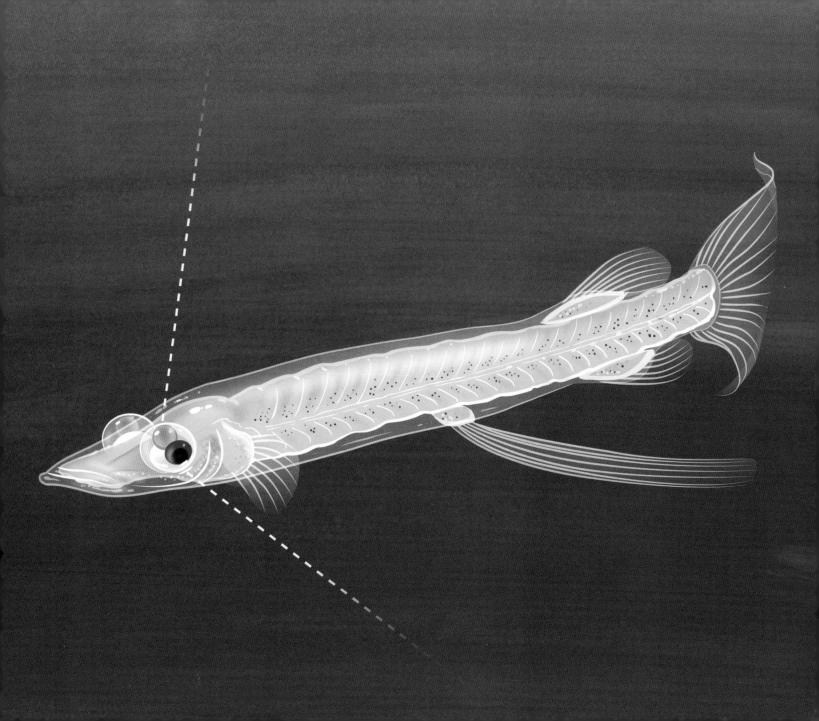

THE COLOR OF PREY

Bees use sight to find flowers with nectar. This is their food. Even if a flower does not look pretty to us, it may attract a bee. Bees can see the flower as a completely different color. And that color looks tasty!

Does the color of food make you hungry?

Looking Straight Ahead

Most predators have eyes on the front of their head. This makes it easy to see their prey.

A cheetah's eyes are set high. They face the front. Like all big cats, a cheetah's pupils are round. They can see faraway objects, such as a deer or other prey.

If you were to look through a pair of binoculars, you still would not see the same detail that a cheetah sees.

20

EYES ABOVE AND ON THE SIDES

A frog's eyes are above and on the sides of its head. A frog can hide underwater with only its eyes sticking out. It can also turn its eyes all around to find food.

The hammerhead shark's eyes stick out from its wide head. This gives it better sight as it glides through the water. A hammerhead shark can see all the way around itself because of where its eyes sit on its head!

The next time you swim, try to look above the water without moving your head. It would be much easier if your eyes were on top and to the side like the hammerhead's!

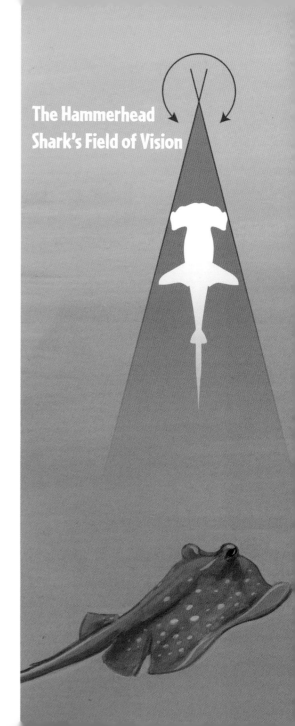

The Hammerhead Shark's Field of Vision

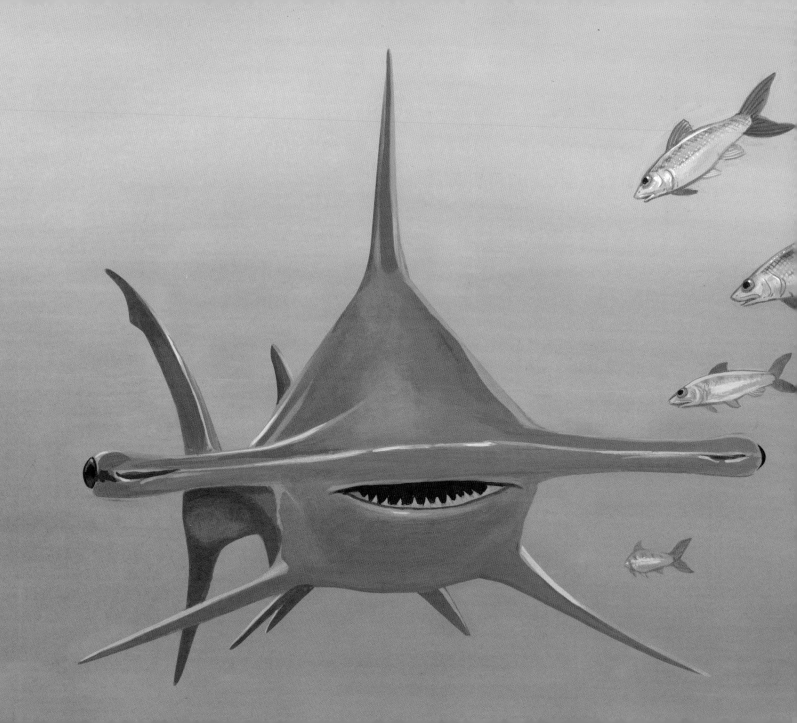

Brain

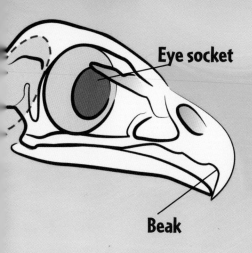

Eye socket

Beak

SEEING CLEARLY

Eagles, hawks, and falcons are raptors. These birds of prey can see up to eight times more clearly than a human!

Raptors have especially large eyes. Large eyes let in the most light and give a bigger image of what they are seeing. A bird's eyes are so big that they take up most of the skull. This gives only a small amount of room for the bird's brain.

Flying birds often hunt small prey on the ground. They must be able to tell the distance, size, shape, position, and motion of its prey. They can see whether it is a rabbit, rat, or snake.

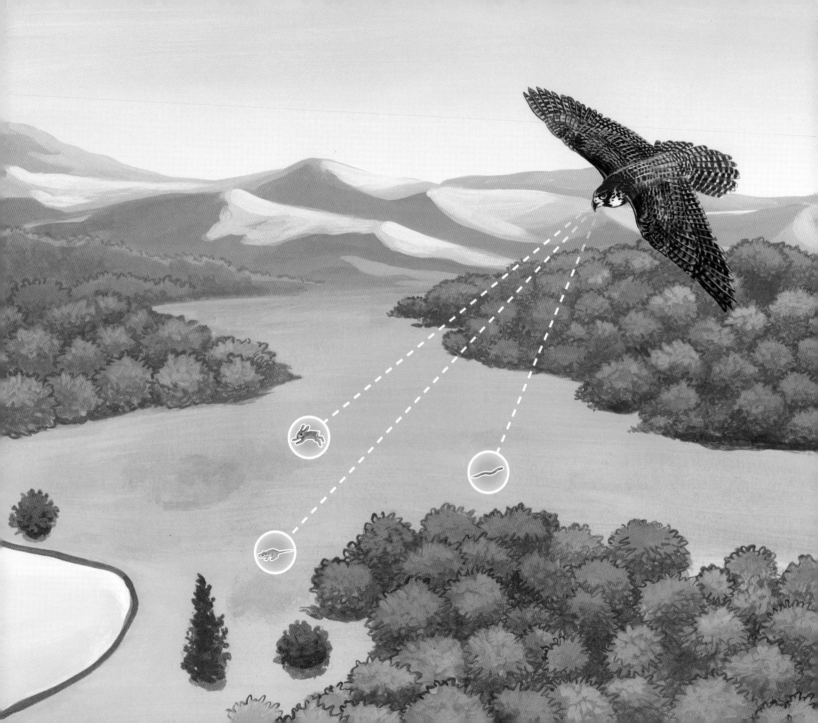

WHEN FOOD HIDES

Insect-eating birds also depend on their eyesight to find prey. Some insects look like leaves, grass, or bark. It is a battle between the bird's eyes and the prey that has found ways to hide. Without their amazing eyesight, many predators would go hungry. Can you see the food on your plate? It must be time to eat!

Glossary

attract - to pull closer.

carrion - dead animals.

nectar - a sweet liquid, or sugar water, that flowering plants make.

nocturnal - active at night.

protection - the act of protecting, or guarding against harm or danger.

pupil - the opening in the eye that lets light in.

telescopic - able to see things that are very far away.

transparent - something that is allows light to pass through.

Index

Web Sites

To learn more about animal senses, visit ABDO Group online at **www.abdopublishing.com**. Web sites about animal senses are featured on our Book Links page. These links are routinely monitored and updated to provide the most current information available.